OVER THE RIVER AND THROUGH THE WOODS

BY JOE DIPIETRO

DPS

DRAMATISTS PLAY SERVICE

OVER THE RIVER AND THROUGH THE WOODS
Copyright © 1999, Joe DiPietro
All Rights Reserved

ISBN 978-0-8222-1712-1
www.dramatists.com
www.concordtheatricals.com

MUSIC AND THIRD-PARTY MATERIALS USE NOTE

IMPORTANT BILLING AND CREDIT REQUIREMENTS

OVER THE RIVER AND THROUGH THE WOODS was produced by Jonathan Pollard, Bernie Kukoff, Tony Converse, and James Hammerstein at the John Houseman Theater in New York City on October 5, 1998. The associate producer was Karen Jason. It was directed by Joel Bishoff; the set and lighting designs were by Neil Peter Jampolis and Jane Reisman; the costume design was by Pamela Scofield; the original music was by Jimmy Roberts; and the production supervisor was Matthew G. Marholin. The cast was as follows:

FRANK	Val Avery
NICK	Jim Bracchitta
AIDA	Joan Copeland
CAITLIN	Marsha Dietlein
NUNZIO	Dick Latessa
EMMA	Marie Lillo

CHARACTERS

NICK CRISTANO .... In his thirties
FRANK GIANELLI ... Nick's maternal grandfather, eighty years old
AIDA GIANELLI .... Nick's maternal grandmother, in her seventies
NUNZIO CRISTANO ... Nick's paternal grandfather, in his seventies
EMMA CRISTANO ... Nick's paternal grandmother, in her seventies
CAITLIN O'HARE ... Attractive and charming, in her late twenties

SETTING

The Gianelli home in Hoboken, New Jersey. Center stage is the living room — the furniture is well-worn, immaculate, and about twenty years out of style. The entrance door leads to the front porch, stage right. Stage left is the dining room, which has two entrances — one leads to the kitchen, the other to the hall.

TIME

Most of the action of the play takes place several years ago.

OVER THE RIVER AND THROUGH THE WOODS

ACT ONE

A spot on Nick, downstage.

NICK. *(To audience.)* It was always hot in my grandparents' house. And I'm not talking "I should've worn short sleeves" hot. No, it was more like "it's August in Ethiopia" hot. Growing up, I remember sitting in their living room, sweating, and trying to figure out my relation to these people who not only didn't seem to share my same environmental needs, but who also had reached an age I could barely comprehend. But my grandparents firmly believed in the three "f's" of life: family, faith and food. So every Sunday for twenty-nine years, I bore the heat and religiously showed up for dinner. *(Lights up on the living room. Frank seated in his usual chair.)*

FRANK. *(To audience.)* The very day I turned fourteen, my father put me on a boat. In my pocket, he stuffed two hundred lira and the address of a cousin in a place called Hoboken, New Jersey. The only advice my father gave me — "*Tengo famiglia.*" If you just said that in English, it would be "I support a family." But in Italian, it means more, much more — "I am a man, I am doing well for my woman and my children, I have a reason for being alive."

NICK. *Tengo famiglia.*

FRANK. *(To audience.)* I arrived to learn my cousin had left Hoboken for a faraway land called Brooklyn. So for six weeks, I lived underneath a pier off the Hudson River — every minute of every day trying to figure out a way to earn enough money to get back home. *(Aida enters.)*

AIDA. *(To audience.)* I was the middle sister of seven girls, and Frank was the first man — no, the first person — to ever notice me. He was making a dollar a day as a carpenter's apprentice, and I thought that was a fortune. He promised that if I married him, he'd become a fine carpenter and he'd build for me — me! — an entire house. And he did. He became a wonderful carpenter, and he built, for me, this beautiful home.

NICK. *(To audience.)* My grandmother Aida never made it through grammar school, never even learned how to drive a car, but lock her in a kitchen with a tomato, pasta dough and garlic, and the woman was Einstein. *(Aida exits.)* By my twenty-ninth birthday, my parents had moved to Florida, and my sister, Melissa, to San Diego. Before she left, Melissa told me that the best thing about being an American is you could stay in the country and still move two thousand miles away from your family. I stayed near my grandparents. Each Sunday, I rode a bus in from the city. But one Thursday, something happened to me — something important — and what I had to tell them couldn't wait. *(Nick enters the living room.)* Hey, Gramps. Hi, Nanny!

FRANK. Nick, your grandmother is going to tell you to do something for her. Refuse! *(Aida enters, giving Nick a hug.)*

AIDA. Nicholas! You have to do something for me. *(Frank motions "no.")* First, you hungry?

NICK. No Nan, I just ate and I can't stay long. Like I said on the phone, I just have to make this announcement.

FRANK. He has no time to do you any favors, Aida.

AIDA. What did you have for dinner?

NICK. Chinese food.

AIDA. Chinese?

NICK. Nan —

AIDA. You're telling me that's food?

NICK. Well, everyone eating it seemed to think so, yes.

AIDA. Thirty years ago, I had dinner at a Chinese restaurant. To this day, I have no idea what I ate. I'll make you food!

NICK. Nan, I'm full!

AIDA. Fine, I'll make you a sandwich.

NICK. Nan!

AIDA. You look hungry!

NICK. How? Tell me exactly how do I look hungry?!

AIDA. You're breaking my heart, Nicholas.

NICK. All right, all right! A small sandwich.
AIDA. What do you want on it?
NICK. I don't care!
AIDA. How about provolone and ham?
NICK. Perfect!
AIDA. Good. Nicholas, I'll make a provolone and ham sandwich, you tell your grandfather he can't drive no more.
NICK. What?!   FRANK. Don't listen to her, Nick!
AIDA. Two days ago in the Grand Union parking lot, he puts the car in reverse and goes forward —
FRANK. I thought it was reverse, I put it in second —
AIDA. Right into a Japanese car. Thank God no one was killed.
FRANK. I barely dented the fender.
AIDA. Two weeks ago at the 7-Eleven, he means to step on the brake, he steps on the gas pedal —
FRANK. We go very fast for about two feet —
AIDA. Right into a Japanese car. Thank God no one was killed.
NICK. Gramps, we've talked about this. You shouldn't be driving anymore.
FRANK. You? You're telling me what to do? I used to change your diapers!
NICK. You've told me, I appreciate it.
AIDA. He never changed your diapers.
NICK. Look Gramps, it's too dangerous with you behind the wheel.
AIDA. I get in the car with him, I scream the entire way.
FRANK. She's a real pleasure to drive with.
NICK. All right, all right — Nan, why don't you make the sandwich? I'll talk to him. And could you turn on the air conditioner. It's sweltering in here.
FRANK. That's crazy! It's only June!
NICK. But it's hot!
FRANK. The air conditioner doesn't go on until the Fourth of July!
AIDA. I'll open a window. You listen to your grandson! *(Aida opens a window, barely a crack, and exits.)*
NICK. Gramps, come on. You know something terrible could happen.
FRANK. I have to drive your grandmother to the store —
NICK. She can walk — take the bus —
FRANK. I only go close by — that's all.
NICK. And you still get into accidents.

FRANK. So what're you saying? I'm too old to drive?
NICK. Your reflexes are just getting a little slow … *(Aida enters.)*
AIDA. I'm out of provolone. Cheddar or muenster?
NICK. Whatever, Nan!
AIDA. I want to make it the way you like it.
NICK. How can you make it the way I like it? I don't even want it!
AIDA. Don't talk fresh. Cheddar or muenster?
NICK. Cheddar.
AIDA. You sure?
NICK. Absolutely, one hundred percent, I want cheddar, Nan.
AIDA. But I got such nice muenster —
FRANK. This is the woman you're listening to so I can't drive!
NICK. All right, Nan, muenster! I want muenster!
AIDA. I thought so. *(Aida exits.)*
NICK. Look — Gramps — I just don't want to get a phone call saying you hurt yourself — or Nan — or someone else. *(A beat.)*
FRANK. My first car — 1941 DeSoto. Cost fifty-three dollars more than I could possibly spend. But once I laid eyes on it — chrome wheels — black leather inside — dashboard that was the most beautiful sight I ever saw. *Bellisima.* I worked three months, nights, shoveling coal into some restaurant furnace, so I could get that fifty-three. And when I bought that car, when I actually sat behind that dashboard, when I held that perfect new steering wheel in my hand — that's when I knew I could make a life for my family. If I could own this car, I could make a life. *Tengo famiglia.* *(Nick holds out his hands. Frank looks at him for a moment, then reluctantly gives him his car keys.)*
NICK. Thank you.
FRANK. I got another set hidden in my tools.
NICK. Just promise you'll only drive in an emergency — all right?
FRANK. Yeah, yeah … *(Emma and Nunzio enter, on the porch.)*
NUNZIO. *(To audience.)* I was the first in my family to get a good job with a union — in a Ford's automobile factory. And the way I got the job, see, was I told them I was Irish. I had to! 'Cause those days, the most famous Italians in America were the Pope, and Sacco and Vanzetti! And did they look at us and think Pope? No! Sacco and Vanzetti!
NICK. *(To audience.)* My father's folks, Nunzio and Emma, lived two doors down, and every Sunday, they'd also visit and share dinner. Both children of hard-working but destitute immigrants, they

married at seventeen and had two sons — my dad, and his brother Nick, who was killed in Korea.

EMMA. *(To audience.)* The day I married Nunz, my mother sat me down and told me something amazing — she said, "Emma, just because you're his wife, it doesn't mean you're not as important as him. Speak up! Say how you feel! Don't become one of those women who gets lost behind their family." Ha!

NUNZIO. *(To audience.)* So I told Ford's my name was Ian Sean O'Malley O'Brien O'Sullivan — and they gave me the job!

EMMA. *(To audience.)* So while Nunz went to work, I made us a beautiful life at home.

NUNZIO. *(To audience)* I stood on an assembly line and put this nut in that bolt for twenty-seven years to give my wife and my sons the life they deserve!

EMMA. *(To audience.)* We struggled and made our way 'cause we were a family! *Tengo famiglia!*

NUNZIO. *(To audience.) Tengo famiglia!*

NUNZIO and EMMA. *Tengo famiglia!!*

NICK. *(To audience.)* They were the loudest people I ever met. *(Nunzio and Emma enter the living room.)*

NUNZIO. Hey Nicky!!

EMMA. Yoo hoo!

NICK. Hi, Nanny. Hi, Gramps.

NUNZIO. What a pleasure to see you on a Thursday!

NICK. I'm glad you came. I have something to tell you.

NUNZIO. Wait Nicky, first I wanna take a picture.

NICK. Of what?

NUNZIO. Of you.

NICK. Why?

NUNZIO. I got two pictures left on this roll since last Easter. Stand by your grandmother and smile.

NICK. Gramps, I got this announcement …

NUNZIO. It's one picture —

NICK. Gramps!

NUNZIO. One picture!

NICK. All right, all right …

EMMA. *(Going for his hair.)* Fix your hair nice first.

NICK. Nan, stop! All right, Gramps — shoot.

NUNZIO. But you don't look happy.

NICK. I'm not happy!

NUNZIO. Why would I take a picture if you don't look happy! *(Nick forces on a smile as Nunzio snaps away.)*
FRANK. Nunz, make me a copy, I'll pay ya for it.
NUNZIO. Okay, I got one more.
NICK. No! Enough with the pictures.*(Calling toward kitchen.)* Nan, could you get back in here, please!
EMMA. Nicky, that present you bought for us. The one we don't know how to use —
NICK. The answering machine?
EMMA. The other one. The CPU —
NICK. VCR —
EMMA. Right. We need the receipt.
NICK. It broke?
NUNZIO. No, we just hate it.
EMMA. We don't hate it! It's just too expensive, we can't enjoy it.
NICK. Why you worried about the expense? I bought it for you.
EMMA. Give us the receipt, we'll give you back the money.
NICK. I don't want the money!
NUNZIO. It's too much to spend on us for a BCP!
NICK. It's your sixtieth anniversary present!
EMMA. Fine, we'll keep ten dollars!
NICK. Look, we'll talk more about this later. I've got something much more important to …
NUNZIO. So Nicky, guess where your grandmother wants to drag me — again! — next Tuesday!
EMMA. I'm sorry if I like to go places and do things. I'm a do-er!
NUNZIO. Atlantic City! With the senior citizens from St. Anne's!
NICK. Gramps, what I have to say is real important. Can we talk about …
NUNZIO. You sit in traffic for four hours with a busload of eighty-year-old Catholics all carrying these giant bags of quarters! It's awful!
EMMA. Listen to what he's complaining about: You get a free, air-conditioned bus ride and they give you thirty dollars free in chips.
NICK. Look, I have this announcement …
NUNZIO. You know what I did last time we went: walked into Donald Trump's, cashed in my thirty dollar chips, found a five buck buffet, ate all day and came home with a twenty-five dollar profit!
EMMA. I've told him, that money was not for him to keep. The

Catholic Church gave him that money to gamble! Sunday, you put it in the poor box —
NUNZIO. I'm not putting it in the poor box, *we're* poor! I'm giving it to Nicky!
EMMA. We are not poor!
NICK. Why are you giving me twenty-five dollars?
NUNZIO. I don't know! She won't let me keep it! *(Aida enters with the sandwich.)*
AIDA. I forgot if you said cheddar or muenster so I put on both.
NICK. *(To audience.)* How did I come from these people? My parents — maybe I can understand. But these people?
AIDA. Nicholas ate Chinese food tonight.
NUNZIO. That's like eating cancer.
FRANK. He also said I can't drive no more.
EMMA. Good. The world just got safer.
NICK. All right, I'll give you the receipt for the *V-C-R*, we'll talk more about the driving, I'll eat the sandwich. Can everyone take a seat, please? I'd like to say what I have to say now.
EMMA. He's getting married!
FRANK. How can he get married? He doesn't even have a girlfriend!
NICK. I'm not getting married!
FRANK. Why not?!
NICK. Look, can we save that argument for the holidays, when we always have it! What I have to say is about something entirely …
EMMA What about Donna?
NICK. No! I will not discuss Donna! That subject is closed! I broke up with her two years ago!
NUNZIO. I thought she broke up with you.
FRANK. She did. He was dragging his feet.
NICK. Can we move on, please?
AIDA. Oh, she had such nice hair.
EMMA. I was so sure you were going to get engaged, Nicky, every time I went to a party, I'd take all the extra plastic knives and forks and save them for your wedding shower. *(The phone rings.)*
AIDA. I'll get it!
NICK. No, Nan! Just let the answering machine get it.
FRANK. No, Nick, that machine broke.
NICK. I just got it for you. How'd it break?
FRANK. I threw it out. Every time we pressed a button, someone was yelling at us.

NICK. That was people leaving messages!

EMMA. Nicky, I want to see you married before I'm dead.

NICK. Tell me when you feel you're going, I'll see who I can dig up. Now …

AIDA. Nicholas, it's your parents! *(Into phone.)* Nicholas ate Chinese food tonight —

FRANK. Nick, why your parents moved to Florida —

EMMA. God only knows! They spend the first fifty-six years of their lives nice and close to their parents —

NUNZIO. — who raised them!

EMMA. Then, boom! Your father gets a little sinus condition, so they retire early and move to Fort Lauderdale —

FRANK. — to live with a bunch of old people who love humidity!

AIDA. Frank, come say hello.

NUNZIO. You're a good boy, Nicky, staying near your family —

AIDA. *(Giving Frank the phone.)* It's long distance, talk fast.

FRANK. *(Into phone.)* Hi, your son told me I can't drive no more. Come visit soon, we'll sit in my car and pretend it's moving. *(He hands the phone back to Aida and returns to his chair.)*

EMMA. Then your sister gets married and moves to San Diego —

NUNZIO. Who the hell moves to San Diego?!

NICK. Nan, Gramps, please! *(Aida hangs up the phone and returns.)*

AIDA. Nicholas, your mother said call her after you tell us. She wants to know if we take it well.

NICK. Well, we'll all find that out in a moment, if everyone can just please sit now.

AIDA. Aren't you going to sit?

NICK. No, I want to do this standing up.

EMMA. It's like he's going to make a speech.

NUNZIO. If he wants to make a speech, let him make a speech.

NICK. It's not a speech! Can I just please say this now?!

AIDA. Before you start — who's hungry? *(Aida crosses to the dining room.)*

NICK. Nan, this is a one-sentence announcement. You don't have to cater it!

AIDA. I got a new crumb cake.

NUNZIO. With the big crumbs?

AIDA. From the A&P.

FRANK. I'm in!

EMMA. I just want a sliver, but a healthy sliver.

NUNZIO. I want a really big piece!

AIDA. Don't announce anything yet, Nicholas.

NICK. Nan! *(Aida rushes into the kitchen.)*

EMMA. Oh Nicky, here, before I forget — I got you a mass card.

NICK. Mass card? Aren't these for sick people?

EMMA. Two Thursdays from now, the 7:30 mass at St. Anne's will be said for you —

NICK. Why?

EMMA. — in hopes you meet a girl to marry.

NICK. And the priest agreed to this?

FRANK. Hey, go to the mass, maybe you'll meet her there.

NUNZIO. If you go, Nicky, whatever you do, don't talk to Father Vicenzo.

EMMA. Not with Father Vicenzo again!

NUNZIO. Hey, fifteen years ago, him and I had a big falling out!

FRANK. About what?

NUNZIO. I don't know. I just remember being right! *(Aida enters and distributes the cake and coffee.)*

AIDA. Okay, here we are —

NICK. Thank God. Can I start now?!

FRANK. Wait! I feel a draft.

EMMA. Me, too. What's open?

NICK. It's a hundred and ten degrees in here!

NUNZIO. We're old, we're chilly.

AIDA. *(Closing the window.)* Oh my lord, I forgot all about it!

NICK. Good thing you got that, Nan. For a moment, you almost let air seep into the room! All right, does everyone have their crumb cake? Does everyone have their coffee? Is anyone disturbed by any unbearable drafts?! *(Nunzio snaps a flash picture of Nick.)*

NUNZIO. Okay, all done.

FRANK. Make me a copy, Nunz, I'll pay you for it.

NICK. Can I please say this now?!

NUNZIO. What's he getting so upset about?

EMMA. He was always anxious. Remember how he used to chew on his rattle.

NICK. Can we not tell the rattle story right now?!

EMMA. We're just trying to understand you better, Nicky.

NICK. Oh, and the rattle story just explains it all! I don't even know why I bother going to therapy!

EMMA. What?
NICK. Nothing! I said nothing!
NUNZIO. He said he's going to therapy.
FRANK. What the hell is that?
EMMA. He's going to a psychiatrist.
FRANK. Foot doctor?
EMMA. Head doctor.
FRANK. What?!
AIDA. Nicholas, you're seeing a head doctor?
NUNZIO. Oh my God!
NICK. Look, it's no big deal. All my friends are in therapy — it's just someone to talk to —
EMMA. What kind of friends do you have, Nicky?
NICK. I said it was no big deal.
NUNZIO. Can't you just talk to us?
NICK. How?! I can't even get this announcement out!
FRANK. Do you pay this person or is it covered with insurance?
NICK. I really don't want to talk about this right …
FRANK. I hope you don't pay this person.
AIDA. We listen to your problems for free.
EMMA. A priest would, too, Nicky. Should I call a priest?
NUNZIO. She's always calling a priest!
EMMA. Shut up, I'm talking to my grandson!
NUNZIO. The other day, my back hurts, I hear her on the phone to the parish.
AIDA. Tell us your problems right now, Nicholas.
NUNZIO. I walk out of the bathroom, Father Fanelli's standing there waiting to bless my spine.
NICK. Look, I'm seeing this therapist, yes! But I won't be seeing him much longer —
EMMA. Thank God!
NICK. And that ties in with my announcement! Can I please tell you now?!
AIDA. Nicholas, go ahead, say your announcement. We're all listening very hard.
NICK. Okay!
FRANK. All right!
EMMA. Everyone quiet!
NUNZIO. Okay!
AIDA. Okay!

FRANK. All right!
EMMA. Okay!
NUNZIO. We're ready!
AIDA. Okay!
FRANK. All right!
EMMA. Say it loud!
NUNZIO. Okay!
AIDA. Okay!
FRANK. All right!
NICK. Okay! Let me start with this — I got offered a promotion at work.
EMMA. Congratulations!
AIDA. Wonderful, Nicholas!
NUNZIO. What kind of promotion?
NICK. Well, um — it's a better management position.
EMMA. Tell — tell!
NICK. I could, but I don't think you'd understand. I mean, you don't really understand what it is I do now —
NUNZIO. Just because we wouldn't understand it, it doesn't mean we don't want to hear about it.
NICK. Okay. Uh — now, as I explained before, I work in marketing, which is kind of like advertising, you know, commercials — but I don't actually make the commercials, I, uh, how should I say — plan overall strategy for commercials, and newspapers ads, and various other types of media such as brochures, billboards and internal and external sales presentations. Well, with my new position, and this is exciting, I'll be in charge of developing, coordinating and implementing all of those strategies in a top twenty market! *(A beat, as they look at him.)*
NUNZIO. Well, whatever the hell it is you do, we're damn proud of ya!

AIDA.	EMMA.	FRANK.
Very nice,	What a job!	*Molto bene!*
Nicholas!	What a job!	*Molto bene!*
Very nice!		

NICK. Now the thing about the job, see, is I, uh, have to move.
EMMA. Out of the city? Oh, thank God!
AIDA. Nicholas, you can move in with us!
FRANK. No rent, four meals a day!
NICK. No, no, the job, uh, the job is in — Seattle. *(A beat.)*

FRANK. Where the hell is Seattle?

AIDA. Rose Ranolli has a beach house there. Exit 94 on the Parkway.

FRANK. No, her house is further down, by the big Foodtown …

NUNZIO. No, no, stop, stop. Stop. *(A beat.)* I know where Seattle is — Washington. Not the close Washington. The faraway Washington by California. All the way by California.

AIDA. Nicholas, is this true?

NICK. It's in Washington state, yes. *(A beat.)* Look, I just got the offer this morning — my head is still swimming. But it's a promotion. And now would be the time — right? I'm young — unattached. So there's nothing really to keep me here. *(A beat.)*

AIDA. What about us?

NICK. Well I mean, yeah, except you.

NUNZIO. Nicky — ?

FRANK. So you're leaving?

NICK. Moving, yes.

FRANK. Right. Leaving.

NICK. I told my parents — they thought it's a terrific opportunity. And besides, I grew up in this area, went to college here. I've never lived anywhere else.

EMMA. I've never lived anywhere else —

NICK. Look, I know this might come as a bit of a shock —

FRANK. Shock?! No, why should this be a shock?! First your parents move to Fort Lauderdale, then your sister moves to San Diego, gets married and has my great-grandson —

NICK. Gramps —

FRANK. My great-grandson! I have one great-grandson and he's three years old and I've seen him exactly twice. Twice!

NICK. Gramps, please!

FRANK. You know what that's like! I've lived long enough to have a great-grandson and he has no idea who I am — why I'm important to him. Last time, we got off the plane, and he saw me standing there — with my arms outstretched — and he ran away. He thought I was just another old person. Another old person who wanted to annoy him with a hug. *(A beat.)*

AIDA. Nicholas, I don't know if I understand? You're just going to go?

NICK. Look, it just came up today, I just wanted to tell you first.

NUNZIO. But your family's here, Nick —

NICK. *(Kissing everyone "good night.")* Look, it's late, I got to catch the next bus back.

EMMA. Nicky — ?

NICK. I got an eight A.M. meeting — about the promotion.

AIDA. We'll see you Sunday, Nicholas.

EMMA. If we're still alive, God willing.

NICK. We'll talk more about it then, okay? *(He begins to exit, then stops.)* It's a wonderful opportunity — *(He exits.)*

NUNZIO. Seattle?

AIDA. He forgot his sandwich.

FRANK. It's a twenty-minute ride into the city. He'll make it without food.

NUNZIO. Seattle?

EMMA. Not to worry. He won't go.

NUNZIO. You heard him. He said he wants to move away.

EMMA. No, he didn't say he wants to move. He said he had no reason to stay.

NUNZIO. So?

EMMA. So — we give him a reason. *(A spot on Nunzio.)*

NUNZIO. *(To audience.)* I should tell him — I should tell him that the doctors did their tests — and it has spread. I should tell him that if he takes the job, when he says good-bye, it'll probably be the last time we see each other. No one knows yet — not even my Emma — I'll tell her — soon. But I should tell him. Then maybe he'd stay. *(A spot on Nick, D.)*

NICK. *(To audience.)* Most companies have this unwritten rule: If you say "no" to a promotion, another one might not come along. That day, my boss had sat me down and said, "This opportunity means that we have great faith in you, this means that we're planning something even bigger." And, as any young man can tell you, the lure of a new life is as seductive as any lover. The following Sunday, I returned for our weekly dinner, at which I expected them to be laying the guilt on something fierce. But they didn't. They did something worse. *(Lights up on the living room. Frank sits, playing a mandolin. Nick enters.)* Hello.

FRANK. Hiya, Nick!

NICK. Since when do you play the mandolin?

FRANK. When I was a little boy, my father taught me. Your grandmother found this at a garage sale the other day, so last night, I took a lesson they were having at the high school.

NICK. The high school? How'd you get there? You didn't drive? *(Frank looks at him, hard.)*
FRANK. I walked. Forty-five minutes. In the dark. There and back. If I dropped dead, I left specific instructions to deliver me to your doorstep. *(Nunzio enters from the kitchen, carrying a bowl of nuts.)*
NUNZIO. Hi, Nicky.
NICK. Hi, Gramps. Hey, what's with the jackets and ties?
NUNZIO. What? We can't dress up to see our grandson?
NICK. So anyway — I suppose my move to Seattle — you've both had time to mull it over — eh?
NUNZIO. Nicky, you want some nuts?
NICK. Uh, no thanks. So how you feeling?
FRANK. We're good, Nick, have some nuts.
NICK. No, how you feeling about my promotion?
FRANK. Oh, we're very proud. *(Aida enters from the kitchen.)*
AIDA. Nicholas! You hungry?
NICK. Nan, about Seattle –
AIDA. We'll be eating soon, why don't you comb your hair a little nicer?
EMMA. *(Offstage.)* Yoo hoo, Nicky!
NICK. Hi, Nan! *(To grandfathers.)* Uh — what's going on? Three days ago, I told you about my promotion, and you were all miserable. Now it's like I never even …
NUNZIO. Hey Nicky, how old are you?
NICK. What? Twenty-nine.
FRANK. Twenty-nine and no family.
NUNZIO. You know, you're eight years older than your Uncle Nicky ever was.
NICK. What? What brought that up?
NUNZIO. Just been thinking of him lately.
NICK. Why?
EMMA. *(Offstage.)* Yoo hoo, Nicky!
NICK. What, Nan?!
EMMA. *(Offstage.)* How does your hair look today?!
NICK. I combed it into an afro, Nan! All right, exactly what is up with you people?
NUNZIO. Who is this "you people"?
FRANK. We're not people, we're your family.
NICK. Look, something's going on, everyone's being too quiet

and … *(The doorbell rings. Emma rushes in from the kitchen and answers it.)*
EMMA. I'll get it!
AIDA. Why, who could that be? *(Emma opens the front door.)*
EMMA. Why it's Caitlin O'Hare, the unmarried niece of my canasta partner, Margaret O'Hare.
NICK. Oh my God …
AIDA. Caitlin, come in — why don't you stay for dinner!
CAITLIN. Hi, Emma. Hi — wow, if I knew there were so many of you, I would've brought two bottles of wine —
EMMA. Oh no, this is so thoughtful. Isn't Caitlin so thoughtful, Nicky?
NICK. I can't believe you're doing this.
EMMA. *(Trying to neaten Nick's hair.)* Caitlin, I want you to meet my beautiful grandson, Nicholas.
NICK. Stop! Caitlin — uh, hi. It's Nick.
CAITLIN. Hi, Nick. Great to meet you.
AIDA. And I'm his other nanny, and if you call her Emma, you call me Aida.
CAITLIN. Absolutely. Hello, Aida.
NUNZIO. Then I'm Nunzio.
FRANK. And I'm Frank.
CAITLIN. Well it's a pleasure to meet you, Nunzio and Frank.
NUNZIO. And you seem like a girl who any young man would be lucky to have as his wife.
NICK. Oh God —
CAITLIN. Nunzio, you're absolutely right.
AIDA. Well Caitlin, you're just in time for supper, everything came beautiful —
NICK. Uh, wait, wait, I, uh, just need to have a moment alone with Caitlin first — *(Grandparents react happily.)*
AIDA. It's working, it's working! *(Nick takes Caitlin aside.)*
NICK. Look, I just want to say — well, did my grandmother happen to mention I'd be here?
CAITLIN. Uh — no. She didn't, no.
NICK. Okay, in case you haven't figured it out yet, this is a blind setup. So feel free to run like the wind —
CAITLIN. Nick, relax. I hate being set up, too. But Emma's my friend, it's no big deal. Besides I gotta say, the dinner smells fantastic.

NICK. That's their secret. They suck you in with the food.
CAITLIN. Well, I don't know about you, but I'm going to stay.
NICK. You sure? 'Cause it's not too late to escape.
CAITLIN. C'mon Nick, we'll just have a, you know, relaxing Sunday dinner.
NICK. Caitlin, even at my most generous moments, I would not describe these people as relaxing. *(Emma crosses to Nick and Caitlin.)*
EMMA. Very pretty, isn't she, Nicky?
NICK. Uh — yes, yes.
EMMA. I did good.
AIDA. Okay, time to eat! Caitlin, you look hungry. Come — *(Emma leads Caitlin into the dining room, followed by Nick.)*
NICK. Oh my God, oh my God, oh my God …
AIDA. Okay, Nicholas why don't you sit next to — Caitlin! *(He does. Grandparents stare happily at them.)* Very nice, very nice.
NICK. Can we just eat now! Quickly!
EMMA. Shall we say grace?
NUNZIO. Since when do we say grace?
EMMA. Shut up, we have company!
AIDA. Frank, say grace.
FRANK. Really? Well all right, everyone get ready, I'm gonna say grace. All right.
EMMA. Everyone quiet!
NUNZIO. Okay!
AIDA. Okay!
FRANK. All right!
EMMA. Okay!
NUNZIO. We're ready!
AIDA. Okay!
FRANK. All right!
EMMA. Say it loud!
NUNZIO. Okay!
AIDA. Okay!
NICK. Say "grace," Gramps!
FRANK. All right. Bless us, oh Lord, for these thy gifts, that we are about to receive. And bless our lovely dinner guest and our lonely grandson and may they find eternal happiness together.
GRANDPARENTS. Amen.   NICK. Gramps!
FRANK. It's a prayer, I could say whatever the hell I want!

EMMA. Caitlin, before I'm dead, I want to see Nicky married.
NICK. If not, I have to go with her. *(Aida exits into the kitchen.)*
NUNZIO. *(Pouring Caitlin wine.)* So Caitlin, I bet you like to drink.
CAITLIN. How do you mean?
NUNZIO. Well, you're Irish —
NICK. Gramps!!
NUNZIO. The Irish like to drink. That's a secret?
NICK. Gramps, apologize now!
CAITLIN. Actually, I don't mind having a pint or two now and then.
NUNZIO. You see? Life is to be lived! You know Caitlin, the Irish used to hate the Italians.
NICK. Okay, change the subject!
FRANK. So Caitlin, tell me — do you drive?
NICK. Gramps —
CAITLIN. Sure. Don't you?
FRANK. Funny you should ask —
NICK. He had to stop. He's been getting into accidents lately.
FRANK. I've killed hundreds of people. *(Aida enters.)*
AIDA. Here we are! Caitlin, I made some lovely veal. Pick a piece.
CAITLIN. Oh Aida, no thank you. I'll just have the vegetables.
AIDA. No, have some veal. It's nice from the Shop Rite.
CAITLIN. Thank you, Aida, but I'm a vegetarian. *(A beat. Grandparents stop and stare at her.)*
NUNZIO. She's a what?
EMMA. Vegetarian.
FRANK. What the hell's that?
EMMA. Animal doctor.
AIDA. Very nice.
FRANK. So she won't eat veal?
NUNZIO. She fixes animals so she don't eat them. Makes sense.
CAITLIN. No, no, "vegetarian" — I don't eat meat. My job is I'm a nurse.
NUNZIO. She's an animal nurse?
FRANK. What do animals need nurses for?
NICK. *(To Caitlin.)* Trust me on this — don't try to correct them, just ride it out.
AIDA. Whatever you do, it sounds very nice. Have some veal.
CAITLIN. Oh I really can't, thank you.

AIDA. No? None at all?

CAITLIN. I'm sorry, Aida, I should've told Emma before I came.

AIDA. Aw, no need to apologize. *(Putting veal on her plate.)* Just have some veal.

NICK. *(Switching plates with Caitlin.)* Nan, the veal issue is closed! She doesn't eat veal!

AIDA. It's from the Shop Rite —

NICK. Nan!

CAITLIN. Aida, that's so sweet of you, but the vegetables really look so delicious. Really, just an extra forkful of those would be wonderful. *(Aida retreats to her seat.)*

NUNZIO. The squash is beautiful from my garden.

CAITLIN. Looks fabulous.

NUNZIO. You could serve it to the Pope.

AIDA. The Pope would eat the veal, too.

FRANK. So Caitlin, tell me, how come a pretty girl like you doesn't have a boyfriend?

NICK. Caitlin, please don't answer that —

CAITLIN. It's okay, Nick, I don't mind. Well Frank, I like to think that it's just that I haven't met the right guy lately.

EMMA. Maybe if you did something with your hair —

NICK. Nan!

EMMA. I meant that nice! *(To Caitlin.)* You know I meant that nice —

NICK. Caitlin, I would just like to take a moment to apologize for — basically everything that's been said this afternoon.

FRANK. What? We said nothing bad! Nunz, did we say anything bad?

NUNZIO. No, we've been delightful.

NICK. Delightful?!

EMMA. Now don't mind Nicky, Caitlin, he just gets a little excited sometimes.

CAITLIN. That's okay. I like passionate people.

EMMA. What a nice way of saying that.

NUNZIO. See, we ain't loud, we're passionate.

EMMA. So Nicky, Caitlin hasn't had a date in a while.

NICK. Nan! That's personal information.

CAITLIN. Actually — she's right.

EMMA. You see Nicky, we had a nice talk about it the other day, right by the produce at Pathmark.

AIDA. What did you buy in produce?
CAITLIN. I don't remember.
EMMA. She bought peppers.
FRANK. Red peppers or green?
AIDA. Never buy red peppers at Pathmark.
NUNZIO. I had a big fight with the manager about the zucchini.
NICK. *(To Caitlin.)* They're talking about food. Get comfortable.
CAITLIN. Actually, the A&P has the freshest zucchini. What I do when I'm working a lot and I don't have time to cook — I sauté a little yellow squash from the A&P, then I melt a very thin slice of provolone over it, and I top it with just a dash of parmesan. You have it with some rye or Italian bread — preferably fresh from Marzoni's Bakery — and it makes the best late night snack. *(A beat. All look at her.)*
FRANK. She's our dream come true!

AIDA.	EMMA.	NUNZIO.
She's perfect, Nicholas, she's just perfect!	Thank you, Lord, Thank you, Lord!	This one's for you, Nicky! This one's for you!

(A spot on Nick.)
NICK. *(To audience.)* The thing which irritated me most is that she actually seems terrific. When your grandmother sets you up, you have every right to be disappointed!
FRANK. So Nick, say something attractive to Caitlin.
NICK. Gramps, please.
EMMA. Nicky has a wonderful job, Caitlin.
NUNZIO. We have no idea what the hell he does, but it's fantastic.
NICK. I'm a marketing executive.
CAITLIN. Oh. Do you enjoy it?
NICK. Yeah, actually I do. Very much.
FRANK. But it's no animal nurse.
EMMA. Frank, shush! Let the kids talk.
FRANK. Sorry. Go ahead you two, pretend like we're not here.
NICK. Oh, like that's possible?!
FRANK. Now he's talking fresh.
NICK. I am not talking fresh.
NUNZIO. He's talking fresh.
NICK. Gramps, quiet —
NUNZIO. I can't be quiet, I'm passionate!
EMMA. So Caitlin, you having a nice time?

CAITLIN. Absolutely.

FRANK. Caitlin, we're so glad you came!

EMMA. You'll have to come again soon. How about next Sunday?!

NUNZIO. We eat together every Sunday. We're a family!

CAITLIN. I have to say, it's actually rather amazing sitting here with all of you, because well, I look at Nick and I think how many grown adults actually get to have dinner with all four of their grandparents?

EMMA. He's a lucky boy.

NICK. It's like hitting the lottery.

AIDA. Caitlin, next time you come for dinner, you bring your grandparents with you.

CAITLIN. Thank you, Aida, but mine have all passed on.

AIDA. Oh, I'm so sorry.   EMMA. Oh, what a shame.

FRANK. But now you have us.

CAITLIN. Why thank you, Frank.

EMMA. So Caitlin, do you go to therapy like Nicky?

NICK. Jesus, Nan!

EMMA. What? I thought you weren't ashamed?

FRANK. Actually, *we're* a little ashamed.

CAITLIN. Actually, I do go. *(A beat. Grandparents look at her.)* For two years now. I like it.

AIDA. But you seem so normal.

CAITLIN. It's an act.

NUNZIO. Nicky says all his friends are in therapy.

NICK. All right, I know it's only the first course, but are there any other personal revelations about me anyone else would like to bring up! Bed-wetting memories? Anecdotes about drooling or…?

CAITLIN. Nick, there's no reason to …

FRANK. Should we tell the rattle story?

EMMA. Nicky was a nervous baby and used to chew on his rattle.

NICK. Isn't that a great story?

NUNZIO. He also got caught in the ninth grade smoking dope.

EMMA. Hey! Keep quiet!

NUNZIO. What? I thought we were telling stories.

NICK. I just want to say that this is working terrifically. From now on, I'm taking you four on all my dates!

CAITLIN. Oh, I'd bet you'd all be great fun on dates. I bet you're all terrific dancers.

NUNZIO. No, but that doesn't stop us! *(Grandparents laugh and start singing and dancing in their seats.)*
NICK. Could someone please pass the salt. And a weapon! *(A spot on Emma.)*
EMMA. *(To audience.)* And so dinner went on. A beautiful meal. We enjoyed the veal, then a fresh tomato garden salad, then ravioli with eggplant on the side, then we had coffee with ricotta cheesecake and fresh-baked anisette cookies. And all through this beautiful meal, I looked at my grandson and the lovely girl sitting next to him, and I thought yes, oh yes, he had found his reason to stay.
CAITLIN. Everything was so delicious, Aida. Thank you so much.
AIDA. Caitlin, tonight for when you're watching TV, let me take the veal and make you a sandwich.
NICK. Nan!
AIDA. *(Rushing into the kitchen.)* No trouble, no trouble …
NICK. Nan, get back here! *(But she is gone.)* Look Caitlin, you don't have to take the veal.
EMMA. What's it gonna do, kill her?
NICK. Nan, please!
CAITLIN. Nick c'mon, it's no big deal, I'll take it.
NICK. Caitlin, you're a guest, you don't have to.
CAITLIN. Yes Nick, I know that —
FRANK. Caitlin, we like you. We hope we see you again soon.
CAITLIN. I really had a great time. You're all so sweet.
NUNZIO. We're old. We're adorable. *(Aida rushes back in with a bag.)*
AIDA. Here we are!
CAITLIN. Thank you, Aida. Good night everybody.

AIDA.	EMMA.	FRANK.	NUNZIO.
It was lovely having you! Come back soon!	Bye! Bye-bye!	Come back any time, sweetheart!	Bye now! Bye-bye!

EMMA. See you at Pathmark! *(Nick and Caitlin exit onto the porch.)*
NICK. Ahhhh! Oh my God, oh my God, oh my God. Okay, first, and foremost, I am so sorry. I mean, deeply, deeply sorry.
CAITLIN. Nick, no, don't apologize for anything, I —
NICK. Look, I feel I owe you something. Something expensive. So how about you let me take you to dinner this week. We can go to a

nice vegetarian restaurant and no one will ask if you're in therapy.
CAITLIN. Nick, I thought you didn't like blind setups.
NICK. No, um, no, I don't. But I, uh, I like you. *(A beat.)* And let me just say, I am really, really normal away from my family. That's right, I'm actually intelligent and somewhat charming, and I'm sensitive — but of course in a very macho sort of way. *(They share a smile.)* So you falling for any of this?
CAITLIN. Uh — maybe.
NICK. Okay, "maybe's" not bad, not bad at all. My grandmother was right. She did good. *(A beat.)*
CAITLIN. Nick, I have a confession to make.
NICK. Oh-oh. You've got a boyfriend, you've got a girlfriend, you're really a man, what?
CAITLIN. Nick, I knew you'd be here today. That's the real reason I came. I've just been, I don't know, feeling a little lonely, maybe even a little desperate — oh my God, I said that word out loud. But yeah, maybe even a little desperate, and I figured — well, since I liked your grandmother so much, maybe she's got a grandson who — well … oh, God —
NICK. Hm. Interesting. Well then, if I may be so bold — what *did* you think of Emma's grandson?
CAITLIN. Well that's the thing. I mean, seeing you with all four of your grandparents, well I was thinking of mine and —
NICK. Right, you said they were all gone.
CAITLIN. I did know my mom's mom, but, what I'm saying is — well — you spent the whole evening yelling at them.
NICK. Oh, that. Well, ya know, family. It's just the way we speak to each other. I take it you and your grandmother didn't speak so …
CAITLIN. No, we never yelled. We used to — talk.
NICK. Talk? I'll have to try that with them sometime.
CAITLIN. Actually, my grandmother used to read to me. But not children's stories, no. You see, after my grandfather died, she started to read these books, these wonderful books, as a way to get through the day without him. When I was about nine years old, she read me *Great Expectations*.
NICK. Wait. She read you Dickens? In its entirety?
CAITLIN. It took six months. And you know how people read to children to put them to sleep? Not my grandmother. She read to enthrall me. And I'd hold onto her so tight, her voice just covering me like a blanket.

NICK. So Caitlin, how about it? Dinner? Tomorrow night? *(A beat.)* You okay?

CAITLIN. Yeah, I, uh — well, seeing you all here — um, my grandmother, when I was thirteen, she, well … I'm sorry, Nick — I can't do this with you —

NICK. What?

CAITLIN. I mean — oh God — you seem like an okay guy, but — but you just acted like such an asshole with them!

NICK. What?!

CAITLIN. Us going out — I'm sorry, I — I …

NICK. Now wait a minute, Caitlin! Caitlin, come on! *(Caitlin quickly exits.)* Wait! So what're you saying then? You're desperate *and* you're turning me down?! Caitlin! *(After a moment, Nick reenters the house. Grandparents are seated, eagerly waiting for him.)*

GRANDPARENTS. Well?! *(Nick begins pacing about the room.)*

NICK. You know — you — you people are unbelievable!

NUNZIO. Again with the "you people"?

EMMA. She turned him down.

NICK. You invited her over without telling me. Which you had no right to …

AIDA. Nicholas, don't get upset. I'll get a fruit bowl.

NICK. No! No food now! Everyone sit and listen to me!

FRANK. You see anyone standing?

NICK. Did any of you take into consideration how I would feel? Did any of you take into consideration how your sneaky little plan — which didn't work, by the way! — was infringing on my life? Hell, no! And exactly what kind of plan was that? You expected what? For us to meet and fall in love and spend the rest of our lives together!

EMMA. Yes!

NICK. Well it doesn't happen that way!

NUNZIO. It happened to us!

NICK. That was a hundred and fifty years ago! Today, we do things different. We have careers and ambitions and we only fall in love with people who *we* choose, who *we* pick, when we're damn good and ready!

EMMA. Well that's the problem right there!

NICK. But no, you people, you just did what you wanted because you want me to live my life your way. Well you know what, maybe I don't want to get married.

FRANK. That's crazy!

NICK. *I'm* talking! Maybe *I* like *my* life the way *I've* made it! Maybe I need to find out what I'm about!

NUNZIO. What?!

NICK. Ya know, now I understand why Melissa and my parents really moved! 'Cause they wanted to live without constant interference! And judgment! And criticism! Oh yeah, I was feeling guilty about going to Seattle — thinking maybe I shouldn't take the job 'cause I'd be leaving you! But now, no guilt! I'm home free! I'm outta here!

EMMA. Nicky!

NICK. In one month I'm gonna get on that plane and fly to a new life! And live the way I want to live! And date the women I want to date — not relatives of my nanny's canasta partner! And I'm gonna go to therapy if I want, and I'm gonna eat all the Chinese food I want! I might even go to therapy and eat Chinese food there! Yeah! 'Cause guess what — and this will be news to you all — but I am an adult! Yes! There is a fully functioning, grown-up man standing before you who is perfectly capable of taking care of himsel — taking care of him — *(Suddenly, he gasps for breath. He clutches his chest, then falls to the ground. Grandparents immediately rush to him.)*

AIDA. NICHOLAS!   EMMA. NICKY!

NICK. — can't breath — can't …

NUNZIO. OH MY GOD, A HEART ATTACK! CALL AN AMBULANCE!

FRANK. No, no! We can get him to the emergency room faster!

AIDA. Nicholas! Nicholas!

FRANK. Emma, get the front door — *(She does.)* Aida, go open the car door — *(She rushes out.)* Nunz, help me carry him — *(Frank holds up car keys.)* I'll drive! (BLACKOUT.)

End of Act One

ACT TWO

Two days later. Frank, downstage.

FRANK. *(To audience.)* So *I* drove Nick to the hospital and I didn't hit anybody or anything. And this was under great strain and stress, 'cause I thought my grandson was having a heart attack. As it turns out, he did have an attack — a panic attack, they called it. The doctors said he had to be in bed for a few days and get rid of everything in his life that was making him upset. So, we figured the only thing to do was to have him stay with us. *(Lights up on the living room. Frank exits. Nick rests on the couch, a blanket covering him. A tray holding the remains of dinner sits nearby.)*
NICK. *(To audience.)* You know that song, "Over the river and through the woods, to grandmother's house we go." It's such a happy song. Those people going to see their grandparents — they're singing and dancing and … *(Aida enters.)*
AIDA. Nicholas, what else can I get you to eat?
NICK. Nan, you've been feeding me nonstop for two days now. But please open a window — it's really hot in here.
AIDA. I don't want you to feel a draft.
NICK. Nan, it's like a sauna, I keep expecting naked fat men in towels to walk by.
AIDA. I'll get you a thinner blanket. Oh, and the other Nanny and Grandpa are coming for cannolis, and Nicholas, before they get here: Seattle — you really might not go, right?
NICK. What?
AIDA. Well, I was thinking, if you were so sure you wanted to leave, you wouldn't have gotten so upset, so sick.
NICK. Wait a minute, Nan, no.
AIDA. All I'm saying, Nicholas, is maybe you're absolutely one hundred percent sure you want to leave. But maybe at the same time, you're absolutely, one hundred percent not sure at all.
NICK. Okay, I'm going to have to hear that one more time.

AIDA. Nicholas, remember what you said when you got sick, when you were yelling, that your parents left because they didn't want to be around us —

NICK. Oh God, Nan, I'm so sorry, I —

AIDA. Nicholas, they didn't leave because they didn't want to be around us. They saw themselves getting old, they saw their lives being spent in one place, and they got afraid of becoming too much like us.

NICK. Nan, no, that's not right. They just wanted to live in sunshine, to —

AIDA. Nicholas, people don't move away from their families because of weather. No, they got afraid. And maybe you are, too.

NICK. Nan, no, no, no, no, no! That's not —

AIDA. Calm, Nicholas, calm. Breathe, good. Okay, maybe I'm all wrong. Okay? Maybe I'm just all wrong. *(She begins to go, then stops.)* But I'm not. *(Aida exits.)*

EMMA. *(Offstage.)* Yoo-hoo! *(Emma and Nunzio loudly enter.)*

NUNZIO.	EMMA.
Hi ya, Nicky! You're looking good!	Nicky! How you feeling!

NICK. Hi, I'm feeling fine.

EMMA. Nicky, you gave us such a fright, collapsing like that —

NICK. I know, Nan —

EMMA. So I got you a mass card. St. Anne's, 10:30, a week from Tuesday.

NICK. They're gonna have to name this church after me soon.

NUNZIO. Don't do that to us again, Nicky. We're old, we're the ones supposed to get sick, not you. *(Aida enters with a blanket. Frank follows her.)*

AIDA. Nicholas was getting hot.

FRANK. No, it's perfect in here. *(Aida and Emma put the blanket on him, meticulously covering him from chin to toe.)*

NICK. Hey everyone, I just wanna say — I, uh, said some things the other day — about leaving and not wanting you to interfere and ...

EMMA. Nicky, you were sick then.

NUNZIO. No one listened to a word you said. *(Aida exits into the kitchen.)*

EMMA. Besides Nicky, I got the perfect way for you to relax — come with us on a vacation. We'll pay!

NICK. I don't know, Nan —

EMMA. Next month, we're taking another one of those Mario Perillo tours!

NUNZIO. Again with the Perillo tour!

EMMA. What? You had a wonderful time last year!

NUNZIO. But you're always going somewhere! You get on the bus, you get off the bus, you take a picture, you get on the bus, get off the bus, take a picture, on the bus, off the bus, take a picture … It was exhausting!

NICK. Nan, I'm supposed to be in Seattle, Nan.

EMMA. *(To Nunzio.)* Maybe he'll meet a nice girl on the tour!

NUNZIO. On a Perillo tour? The girls are all eighty years old!

EMMA. Mario Perillo is Mr. Italy!

NICK. You know, I don't think this trip is going to relax me.

FRANK. Nick, you rest here a few more weeks, nice and quiet, then you think about the trip and Seattle some more.

NUNZIO. So what should we do tonight?

EMMA. Just nothing that gets Nicky too excited.

FRANK. Nick, let's play that game you gave us we don't understand — what's it called?

NICK. Trivial Pursuit.

FRANK. That's it. You have to answer things. *(Frank retrieves the game.)*

EMMA. You feel up to playing a game like that, Nicky?

NUNZIO. No, he'll drop dead from the excitement.

EMMA. Shush!

NICK. Look, I'm fine. You wanna play? Let's play. *(Nick sets up the game as Aida enters and distributes the cannolis.)*

EMMA. Nicky, guess who I saw at the deli counter in Pathmark this morning? Caitlin O'Hare!

NUNZIO. Terrific. Last time you brought her here, you almost killed the boy.

EMMA. She's still very nice, Nicky. And her aunt is a wonderful canasta player.

NICK. That's exactly what I look for in a woman. Can we just play, please?

AIDA. Whatever you want, Nicholas.

NICK. How 'bout teams are you and me, Gramps — *(Indicates Frank.)*

FRANK. Okay Nick, you roll the dice and play the game for us.

We'll just come up with the answers. *(Nick rolls the dice and moves the pieces.)*
NICK. Okay, you're on green.
FRANK. All right, green.
EMMA. Everyone quiet!
NUNZIO. Okay!
AIDA. Okay!
FRANK. All right!
EMMA. Okay!
NUNZIO. We're ready!
AIDA. Okay —
NICK. Read the question, Gramps! Science and nature.
FRANK. All right, green question. All right. *(Reading.)* "What is the process by which plants form — carbohydrates? — when they are exposed to light?"
NUNZIO. What the hell kind of question is that?
FRANK. That's what it says.
NUNZIO. Too hard, give us another.
FRANK. Okay, "Who starred with …"
NICK. Wait, wait, wait! That's the whole point! If you can't answer the question, you lose your turn.
NUNZIO. But what the hell kind of question was that?!
NICK. It was a science question!
NUNZIO. It was about a plant!
FRANK. Look, it's the first question, they're not thinking hard yet. We'll give them another just for now.
NICK. Good point. I forgot the "not thinking hard yet" factor.
FRANK. Okay, here's a nice one. "Who starred with Grace Kelly in *High Noon*"?
AIDA. That is a nice one.
EMMA. Uh — that actor.
NUNZIO. Right. The one with the ears.
AIDA. I always liked him.
FRANK. That's right. Go again.
NICK. Wait, stop! That's the answer on the card? The one with the ears?
FRANK. No, but I know who they mean!
NICK. But they have to tell you who they mean! That's the game! That's why it's fun! That's the whole point of … *(Emma and Aida re-cover Nick with the blanket.)*

EMMA.   AIDA.
Nicky, calm down,   Breathe, breathe, breathe —
calm down, don't
have another attack.
EMMA. Okay, we'll think of who the guy with the ears is. Okay?
Okay, nice and calmly — who the hell's the guy with the ears?
AIDA. Didn't Humphrey Bogart have ears?
NUNZIO. Uh — he dated Lana Turner.
EMMA. Right. Jimmy Stewart!
NUNZIO. Jimmy Stewart didn't date Lana Turner.
EMMA. No?
NUNZIO. No! Jimmy Stewart was married to the woman with
the hair.
EMMA.   No, that wacky guy with the nose was married to the
woman with the hair.
NUNZIO. No, that was the other woman with the hair. Jimmy
Stewart was married to the woman with the hair with the face.
EMMA. Didn't the woman with the face marry that guy with
the face?
NUNZIO. No, that was the guy with the feet.
EMMA. Then who dated Lana Turner?
NUNZIO. That gangster she killed — uh, somebody somebody.
EMMA. No, her daughter killed the gangster with the butcher
knife.
NUNZIO. Yes, the daughter with the butcher knife!
EMMA. That's right!
NUNZIO. Yes!
AIDA. Very nice.
EMMA. That's right! *(A long beat.)*
NUNZIO. What was the question again? *(Nick reacts.)*
EMMA. I remember the question — *"High Noon."*
NUNZIO. Yes, the guy with the ears — what's his name —
Gone with the Wind —
EMMA. — Clark Gable!
NUNZIO. Clark Gable!
FRANK. Very good, Clark Gable.
AIDA. Very nice.
NUNZIO. *(To Nick.)* Happy?
NICK. No, Clark Gable was not in *High Noon*!
FRANK. Get out of here, he was!

NICK. Did you read the back of the card?
FRANK. *(Reading the card.)* Gary Cooper. *(Grandparents look at each other.)*
GRANDPARENTS. Nooooooo!
FRANK. Clark Gable and Lana Turner. Go again. *(A spot on Aida.)*
AIDA. *(To audience.)* When Nicholas was in the hospital, I wished there was something wrong with him —— not something terrible, God forbid, but something wrong enough so he had to stay, so he couldn't leave us, so I could take care of him. You want to help them. So much. Like you did when they were little. It doesn't matter how old they get. You just always want to help them.
FRANK. *(Reading a question.)* Okay, "What author was appointed U.S. ambassador to Spain in 1842?"
AIDA. Oh, my.
EMMA. Give us another.
NUNZIO. No wait, wait, I know this!
EMMA. You do not!
NUNZIO. Yes! When you and that Mario Perillo dragged me to Spain, they had this little statue about this guy. I know this!
EMMA. What's the answer?
NUNZIO. Okay, who's your girlfriend who married that fellow who steals cars?
NICK. What?
EMMA. You mean Irene?
NUNZIO. Right, now what's Irene's sister's name?
NICK. Gramps, do these questions have any vague sort of point?
NUNZIO. Shut up, you're sick! Okay, Irene's sister's name?
EMMA. Which one?
NUNZIO. The one who drinks.
EMMA. They all drink!
NUNZIO. The one who's not fat.
EMMA. Irma.
NUNZIO. Okay, now remember when we saw Irma at the Shop Rite when they were having that special in frozen foods — buy two, get one free —
EMMA. That was Foodtown.
NUNZIO. No, Shop Rite!
EMMA. Foodtown has the buy two, get one free specials. Shop Rite has the double coupon days.
NUNZIO. No, Pathmark has the big fish in the window!

NICK. Gramps!

NUNZIO. Okay, okay. Remember — what was her name? — Irma, she was with some guy, and we were both amazed, 'cause she wasn't drunk and the guy had no teeth?

EMMA. Yeah?

NUNZIO. Now what was that guy's name?

EMMA. Uh — something something.

NUNZIO. Yes, it was Jewish! A Jewish name! What's a Jewish name?!

EMMA. Aida, who do we know that's Jewish?

AIDA. I think Henny Youngman's Jewish —

FRANK. We know Henny Youngman?

NUNZIO. No, it's a name like Henny Youngman but different! Who else?!

EMMA. Sid Caesar!

NUNZIO. No!

EMMA. Milton Berle!

NUNZIO. No!

FRANK. Shecky Green!

NICK. Gramps, you know the answer!

FRANK. I'm caught up in the excitement!

AIDA. Is Merv Griffin Jewish?

NUNZIO. Wait! That's close! Merv — Mervin — Merving — Irving! That's it! That's the guy Irma was with — Irving! *(Grandparents react happily.)*

NICK. So?!

NUNZIO. The ambassador — Washington Irving.

FRANK. That's right!

NICK. *(Laughing.)* That was the most amazing thing —

EMMA. Hey, Nicky! You're laughing!

NICK. Yeah?

EMMA. You've been so worried lately, I don't remember the last time I saw you laugh.

NICK. C'mon!

FRANK. She's right, Nick.

AIDA. Wonderful, Nicholas.

EMMA. When we were your age, Nicky, we always laughed all the time. We didn't have much of anything, but we were always laughing. We always had fun. You take things too hard, Nicky.

NUNZIO. Leave the boy alone, Emma.

EMMA. No. We've all been quiet, saying nothing, 'cause we don't want to upset him. But I'm his Nanny and I want to tell him something.

NUNZIO. She's gonna give him another attack —

EMMA. Shush! Nicky, I think you expect too much. You go looking for the perfect girl, so you find no one. You spend so much time worrying about so much — your job, where you live, what it means — you just expect too much.

FRANK. Listen to your grandmother, Nick.

EMMA. That's right. Because we never expected like you expected, Nicky. We were told a good life is when you find a husband and have kids and you put food on the table and send your kids to school and you don't die doing it — that's a good life. Then we went ahead and told our kids that they can have so much more — they can go to any school they want, have any job they want, meet wonderful people. And maybe that's the way it should be. And you already have much more than we ever had and we are so proud. But then you gotta go to a head doctor and the whole family moves away from each other. And we never had to do that. So did we make a better life for you? It's not a worse life. But better? Just different, maybe. *(A beat.)* See, he didn't have an attack.

AIDA. Enough with the game. Who's hungry?

FRANK. I need some danish.

NUNZIO. Wait. I want to tell a story.

AIDA. Okay, let me just get the danish —

NUNZIO. No, this story is so good, you don't even need food.

FRANK. There's no such thing.

EMMA. What story you talking about?

NUNZIO. The story of how I won you.

EMMA. Stop! No one wants to hear that old …

AIDA. No, tell it.

EMMA. They've heard it!

FRANK. But he always changes it! Tell us, Nunz.

NUNZIO. Nicky, you want to hear it?

NICK. As long as it won't get me too excited.

NUNZIO. All right. Now Nicky, your grandmother lived in this fourth floor walk-up not far from here, and every night I'd climb over this fence, sneak into her backyard, and serenade her.

EMMA. This is not true.

NUNZIO. Would you let me tell my story?!

EMMA. Story is right. I never met him! His father dragged him to my house, my father talked to him, his father talked to me, then both fathers told us we were getting married!

NUNZIO. It happened sixty years ago! Can't I just tell it the way I like it?! All right, the first time I saw her was on a street corner —

EMMA. Hm!

NUNZIO. Yes, it was a beautiful day — beautiful sunshine — and she was waiting for a bus.

EMMA. I was the most gorgeous, eligible, popular girl in the entire neighborhood.

NUNZIO. What?

EMMA. If *you're* telling the story the way *you* want, I'm telling the story the way I want.

NUNZIO. All right. So once I laid my eyes on your grandmother — well, there was something about her — she was smiling, and I had never seen anything so amazing. She was so beautiful, you could drink her from a glass.

EMMA. I was wrong. Every word of this is true.

NUNZIO. Naturally, I couldn't speak to her — I just watched her get on the bus. But then I waited there, all day, till another bus returned her to that spot. And when she strolled home, I followed her and stood right underneath her window. I did this every night for a month — every night for a month, I sang her this one song: *(He sings the first line of an old song from their youth.)*

FRANK. Wait! Let me get my mandolin!

NUNZIO. *(Sings a bit more of the song.)* The night she came down, I was still too nervous to say words to her, so I just kept on singing. *(Nunzio resumes his singing as Frank joins in with his mandolin. Nunzio offers his hand to Emma; she accepts and they dance. Aida rises and dances by herself, singing along with the other grandparents. A spot on Nick. As he speaks, the mandolin playing and singing continue softly.)*

NICK. *(To audience.)* Whenever I see an old, old black and white movie, I can't help but think that that's what things were like in my grandparents' day — that they lived these very black and white lives, and they were all very serious, very earnest, rather joyless. But sometimes — not very often, but definitely sometimes they gave me a glimpse of what they were really like — and suddenly their past would be splashed with color. I'd get a peek at them when they were young and sexual and their whole lives were laid out before them.

AIDA. Nicholas, I need a partner! *(Nick dances with Aida as all sing one final verse of the song, ending with a flourish.)* Who's hungry?
NUNZIO. *(To Emma.)* How 'bout you and me going home now?
EMMA. Nicky, you mind if we leave you early?
NICK. No, go —
EMMA. This is the reason I want you married, Nicky. This is the reason.
NUNZIO. Aida, Frank, see you tomorrow — *(Emma and Nunzio, with a little extra spring in his step, exit, singing.)*
AIDA. Well, I should clean up — *(She begins to go, but Frank grabs her hand. For an extended moment, they kiss. Then Aida exits into the kitchen.)*
FRANK. You feeling better, Nick?
NICK. Yeah, I'm fine, Gramps. It's funny — I can't remember when I've seen you all like that.
FRANK. 'Cause you're never here, Nick.
NICK. What're you talking about? I'm here every Sunday.
FRANK. Yeah, every Sunday — like a habit — like going to church. You're never here, Nick. *(A beat.)*
NICK. Hey Gramps, how about another story?
FRANK. Ah, I can't tell stories like Nunz —
NICK. No, I mean one that's all true. Tell me — tell me what was it was like to leave your family.
FRANK. Why do you want to know that, Nick?
NICK. He was a fisherman, right? *(Frank nods.)* Why did he make you leave?
FRANK. You know the problem with old stories, Nick? You tell them and you realize that people don't change, people do the same things over and over again. When I was a little boy, every Christmas morning, on the cobblestones in town, there would appear this — this sea of vendors — their carts covered with toys — and what I remember most, is the colors — bright reds and blues and oranges — like a rainbow of toys. And my father would carry me in his arms and take me to the first cart, and he'd point to some tiny, dark toy, while I'd point to the biggest and most colorful, but my father would shake his head "no" and we'd move on to the next. And I'd point to another beautiful toy, and he'd shake his head again, and we'd move on. And we'd do that again and again until we had gone to each cart. And then he'd buy me some little gray toy I barely

wanted, and I'd start crying, and he'd carry me back into our house. I always resented him for that — hated him for that. And when I was fourteen, my father put me on a boat to America and said "good-bye, that's where you're gonna live." I was fourteen. I hated him for that, too. Not long after that, he got tangled in a fishing net that was being thrown in the water, and his head hit the side of the boat and they never found him. Eight years from the day he sent me away, I returned to my hometown so my mother and sisters could meet my new family. It was during the holidays, and on Christmas morning, I took your mother in my arms and carried her outside and there they were — all the vendors, like they never left — with all their blue and red and beautiful toys. And your mother pointed to the brightest and prettiest, and any one she'd point at, I bought for her. And when we came back in, our arms full with this — this rainbow of toys, my mother took one look and said: "That's what your father wished he could do! But we barely had enough to buy food on Christmas. That's why he had to send you away. So you could make for yourself a life he could never give you." I always thought my father was a bastard who wouldn't give me anything. Turns out — he was giving me all he had. *(A beat.)* You're going away — aren't you, Nicholas? *(A beat. Crossfade to Nunzio, D.)*

NUNZIO. *(To audience.)* There's a moment when I wake up each morning and I don't remember I'm sick. It lasts only a few seconds, but it's like a little gift I get at the start of each day. That night, I told my Emma. The first time I cried about it, was when she began to cry. I made her promise not to tell anyone — that's for me to do. It would be so selfish of me to tell him. So selfish. But when you get to be my age, you realize what matters is family. What matters is family. And what's in Seattle? Just some job — *(Lights up on Nick, resting on the couch. Caitlin appears on the doorstep and rings the bell. Nick answers the door. He stands there for a moment, stunned.)*

CAITLIN. Hi there, Nick.

NICK. Hi.

CAITLIN. How are you feeling?

NICK. Me? Uh, fine, fine.

CAITLIN. Uh, could I come …?

NICK. Oh yeah, yeah! Come in, come in! I'm wearing my grandfather's pajamas but sure, um …

CAITLIN. I hope I'm not intruding, Nick, but I bumped into Emma the other day —
NICK. Right. At Pathmark or Foodtown, no, Pathmark has the big fish in the window — I've been here too long.
CAITLIN. And she said that after I left, you collapsed.
NICK. Yeah — yeah, that's true. Boy, that's difficult to explain.
CAITLIN. She said you had a panic attack because I rejected you.
NICK. I love that woman.
CAITLIN. I'm sorry, Nick. I hope it really wasn't because of me —
NICK. Oh no, no —
CAITLIN. 'Cause when guys ask me out, I usually don't call them an asshole.
NICK. Good, you probably get more dates that way. *(Aida enters.)*
AIDA. Caitlin!
CAITLIN. Aida, hello.
AIDA. What a wonderful surprise! You look hungry.
NICK. She has this remarkable sense —
AIDA. Let me fix you something …
CAITLIN. Oh no, no, thank you, Aida, I just came by to see how Nick was doing.
AIDA. Oh, he's much better. He just gets nervous.
NICK. I used to chew on my rattle.
AIDA. I'll just fix you a little something …
CAITLIN. No really, Ai —
AIDA. *(Exiting.)* No trouble, no trouble …
NICK. You have three minutes before she comes back with a fully dressed twelve-pound butterball turkey.
CAITLIN. I am sorry about the other day, Nick. You didn't deserve what I said. It's just that well — you see, Nick, when I was thirteen and my grandmother was in the midst of reading me *The Old Man and the Sea* — well, some days I'd visit and she'd read with such excitement and joy and other days she wouldn't let me in the door because she didn't think she knew me. She would stand there in a panic, screaming at me to leave her alone, her eyes darting back and forth —
NICK. I'm sorry —
CAITLIN. That look in her eyes still haunts me and — I'm sorry, too, Nick. I should've told you that the other day. *(A spot on Nick.)*
NICK. *(To audience.)* I don't know what it was — maybe the way the light was hitting her face or the way she was standing or

maybe it was because a woman who had rejected me came back to apologize. I don't know. But at that moment, she struck me as the most intelligent and beautiful woman on the planet, and I wanted her to like me so much. And for a second I had a horrible thought: Could my grandmother actually be right? Do I not really want to move? Could all I need to be happy is the right woman? Oh my God —

CAITLIN. So Emma said you might move to Seattle soon. She said you have a job offer —

NICK. A promotion, actually. A terrific one.

CAITLIN. Great. You know anyone there?

NICK. No. Just the promotion.

CAITLIN. Well, then — *(A beat.)*

NICK. Yeah — *(A beat.)*

CAITLIN. Well, I'm glad you're okay, Nick. I have to go, I'm on shift in half an hour and I can't be late. There are sick animals who need nursing, so —

NICK. Caitlin —

CAITLIN. Yes?

NICK. I'd still like to — I know you already said "no" but — I'd still like to take you out. You know, a real date. No relatives.

CAITLIN. But — you're leaving? For Seattle?

NICK. I've been thinking about not going. I maybe should stay — I don't know.

CAITLIN. Well, what happens if we go out, and we find out we like each other, and you decide to move?

NICK. I — I don't know. I, um … *(A beat.)*

CAITLIN. I really have to go, Nick. The date offer was nice, but, oh, I don't know, I'd just sit there the whole time hoping I didn't like you. That's just too weird. Okay, take care of yourself. *(Caitlin begins to exit. Nick sings the first line of the old song that Nunzio sang earlier. Caitlin stops. A beat. Nick quickly sings a couple more lines of the song.)* Excuse me?

NICK. If that song worked, it's golden.

CAITLIN. Wow. All right, all right, Nick, if you decide not to go to Seattle — all right, call me, and a date with no relatives, you're on. But if you decide to go — then go. Start over. Sometimes you just have to be a little selfish. *(She kisses him on the cheek.)* You know something — just now, when I didn't immediately agree to go out with you — that was probably one of the most mature things I've ever done. *(She exits. Aida enters carrying a huge antipasto.)*

AIDA. Here we are! *(A spot on Emma, D.)*

EMMA. *(To audience.)* Nunzio and I have been together for fifty-five years. Close your eyes and imagine that — fifty-five years. That's what Nicky doesn't understand — by trying to plan out his life so much, by staying away from marriage — he missed that. He'll never know what that's like — how love can deepen to places you've never imagined. Fifty-five years. *(Lights up on the living room. Emma and Aida set the table as Nunzio reads the paper and Frank plucks away on his mandolin.)*

AIDA. Nunz, how about another pillow?

NUNZIO. No, I'm fine —

AIDA. No, let me get you another …

NUNZIO. Stop, I'm fine — *(Nick enters.)*

NICK. Hello.

NUNZIO.	EMMA.
There you are, Nicky!	Oh, thank God!
We're starving!	

AIDA. Nicholas, why you so late?

EMMA. God forbid, we thought you had an attack on the bus!

FRANK. Good thing I was here to entertain the crowd for ya, Nick.

NICK. Sorry, I had a special session with my psychia — uh, head doctor this morning. We had a lot to talk about.

EMMA. Did you talk about your panic attack?

NICK. Yeah —

NUNZIO. And what'd he tell you?

NICK. To calm down.

FRANK. And for that, you paid him money?

AIDA. Enough! Dinner's waiting, everything came beautiful. *(Grandparents cross to the dining room.)*

NICK. Uh, before we eat, I have something to say.

NUNZIO. Talk and eat! You're late. *Mangiamo!*

NICK. It's important. It's about Seattle. *(Grandparents stop and turn toward Nick. They return to the living room and sit.)*

NUNZIO. Go ahead, Nicky.

NICK. Okay, first I want to say, last week, when I spent those days here — that was a real special time for me. It just seemed — I dunno — like maybe we talked a little more than we ever had. Like maybe we connected a little better. I'm not sure …

AIDA. It was beautiful to have you here, Nicholas.
NICK. And I'm getting older, and so are you, and I'd really, really like us to spend more time together like that.
EMMA. Nicky! You're staying!
NICK. I'd really like us to spend more time together like that — in the next few weeks. I am taking the promotion. I leave in a month. *(A beat.)*
EMMA. Nicky —
NICK. It won't be so bad, you know. It's not a terrible plane ride. You can all come visit all you want. The promotion — it's too good, I've worked so hard for it. It could be the start of something so exciting for … *(He stops.)* I — I just would appreciate if you could all understand. *(A beat.)*
AIDA. No. No, I don't understand, Nicholas. I don't —
NICK. Nan —
AIDA. How can you, Nicholas? We're here, Nicholas. Everything is here. How can you just leave your family like that? Why does everyone get so afraid? How can you, Nicholas? Aren't we worth staying for? How can you leave? How can you just leave? How can you just leave?! *(Aida runs off into the kitchen.)*
NICK. Nan! Gramps, you know the last thing I'd ever want to do is hurt Nan or you or …
FRANK. What do you want me to say now, Nick?! Huh?! Stay, please don't leave us! Go, you have my blessing! I can't say any of that, Nick. I can't!
NICK. Gramps, please …
FRANK. Because no matter what I say, what anyone says, you're going to leave us. Everybody goes! I wish I could be more like my father. I wish I could just stand on the shore and watch you sail away and know it's for the best. But I'm sorry, Nick, I can't! I worked all my life so my family … my family … I'm not good with saying things, Nick. I just don't want you to go. *(A beat.)* Nunz? *(Nunz looks up at Frank, then turns his head away.)* Your grandmothers made for us a beautiful meal. *Mangiamo. (Frank exits into the kitchen. A beat.)*
EMMA. Nicky, your grandfather has something he has to tell you —
NUNZIO. Emma!
EMMA. He has to tell you this, Nicky —
NICK. What, Gramps, what is it? Is something … *(Nunzio*

motions for Nick to go to the porch. Nunzio and Emma exchange a look, then Nunzio follows Nick out.) What is it, Gramps? Is something wrong?

NUNZIO. Nicky, what I have to tell you — I have to … *(A beat.)* Nicky, remember when I told you I've been thinking about your Uncle Nicky lately.

NICK. Yeah.

NUNZIO. Well, I been thinking about him 'cause — well I been thinking about when we had to say good-bye. Strange, you know, he would've been in his fifties now, but I can only think of him as young. I always think I should be able to picture him as older, having lived the life he should've lived. But no, all I can see is this young, perfect man, waving good-bye in his uniform. And I knew how dangerous Korea was, oh I knew that. Still I just stood there and waved back, but inside, inside I was wishing so hard that there was something I could say or do, anything, anything, anything at all, that would make him stay. But there was nothing, Nicky, nothing. But now you're leaving, Nicky, and … *(A beat.)* Nicky, let me ask you something first. And tell me the truth, Nicky. Tell me the truth.

NICK. I will.

NUNZIO. Okay. Right before you had your attack that day, when you were yelling, you said something — it had to do with you wanting to find out what you were about or something —

NICK. I was upset then, Gramps, I didn't mean what I was saying —

NUNZIO. No Nicky, one thing I've learned, when people get upset, that's when they mean what they say. What did you mean by that? *(A beat.)* Tell me, Nicholas.

NICK. I'm not sure, Gramps. I guess — I've grown up here, my whole life has been spent here, with you. And — and it's wonderful. It's all so wonderful and I'm so grateful. But I — I just don't need it anymore. I'm sorry if that sounds awful but — I just don't. I need to make my life something of my own doing. There's an opportunity for me in Seattle — a chance to give myself more. God, I'm sorry if that sounds selfish or ungrateful or …

NUNZIO. So Seattle, then. This is not just about a job — it's something you feel you have to do. To make your life. To be happy.

NICK. Yes. Yes. I'm sorry, I …

NUNZIO. And you know this. You know this as much as you know anything.

NICK. Yes, Gramps, absolutely. I'm sor —
NUNZIO. Okay, then. Okay, then. *(Nunzio begins to cross back to the living room.)*
NICK. Gramps — what you had to tell me?
NUNZIO. No. Nothing.
NICK. But you said …
NUNZIO. What I had to say, Nicholas, what I had to tell you — I will always be there with you. *(A beat.)* So you be good! *(Nunzio smiles at Nick for a moment, then enters the living room. He looks at Emma, and shakes his head "no.")*
EMMA. No, we have to tell him, we —
NUNZIO. He has to go, sweetheart. He has to go.
EMMA. But — but —!
NUNZIO. I know. I know all that. But he has to go. *(Nick enters.)*
EMMA. Nicky!
NICK. Nan? *(She looks at Nick, then at Nunzio, then back at Nick. A beat.)*
EMMA. Dinner came beautiful. *Mangiamo.*
NICK. Nan, is there something —? *(A beat.)*
EMMA. Nicky — I really thought you had a chance with Caitlin. I really did. *(Emma extends her hand to Nunzio, and he grasps it, and kisses it. They exit into the dining room. A spot on Nick.)*
NICK. *(To audience.)* With all the hassles that changing both jobs and cities bring, I had little time to spend with them those final few weeks. And that last Sunday seemed to arrive so quickly. I wish I knew what the formula was — How much do you owe those who care for you? How can you repay someone for their devotion? Can it ever be enough? *(Lights up. Dinner has just been eaten. Emma and Aida clear the remaining plates off the table. Nunzio and Nick enter the living room. Nick's carry-on luggage rests near the door.)*
NUNZIO. Nicky, I hope you noticed — in your honor, your grandfather put on the air conditioner today.
NICK. Yeah, I thought I could breathe.
AIDA. Was a beautiful meal, wasn't it, Nicholas?
NICK. Stunning, Nan.
EMMA. We made all your favorites — gnocchi, veal parmesan, tiramisu, biscotti. You're not gonna get a meal like that in Seattle, Nicky.
NICK. *(He smiles.)* I know that, Nan. Nan — I'm sorry, Nan.

EMMA. For what?

NICK. For leaving and for, well — I don't know.

EMMA. Nicky, honey — no, you're not sorry.

NICK. No Nan, I am, I am —

EMMA. Maybe you feel bad for us, because you love us, but you're not sorry. And I think that's good. You have a wonderful life ahead of you in Seattle — why waste time being sorry? If I was sorry for every sad thing that happened in my life, I wouldn't be able to get out of bed anymore. One thing I know for sure, Nicky, you can't keep the people you love most around forever. You can pray and you can scream and you can cry — but you can't keep them forever. Funny, ya know, I never really thought you looked like your Uncle Nicky much. You were named for him, but I couldn't really see him in you. But now I look at you and — you look exactly like him. Just try to be happy, Nicky. Okay? There's nothing for you to be sorry about. *(Aida enters.)*

AIDA. So Nicholas, did your grandfather tell you?

NICK. What?

AIDA. He's selling the car!

NICK. No, he didn't mention …

AIDA. He tried driving to his mandolin lesson the other night and he dented the back fender — guess how? Pulling out the garage. Didn't even make it to the street. Thank God no one was killed! *(Aida exits into the kitchen.)*

EMMA. Oh and Nicky, before I forget, I got you another mass card.

NICK. I wouldn't have left town without one, Nan — *(Frank enters and crosses to his chair.)* Gramps — Nan just told me — you're selling the car.

FRANK. I'm bored with driving.

NICK. That's terrific, Gramps. I would've been worried about you.

FRANK. Don't. Don't you ever worry about me.

NICK. Well — the taxi should be here any minute. *(Aida enters, carrying a large pan.)*

AIDA. Nicholas, for the plane trip, I made you a lasagna.

NICK. Nan, I can't take a lasagna on the plane.

AIDA. Why not?

NICK. I don't know. It just seems like something you can't do.

AIDA. Fine, I'll mail it to you.

NICK. You're gonna put a lasagna in the mail?

EMMA. I just mailed your sister twelve pounds of fettuccine alfredo.

NICK. All right, all right — *(Car horn beeps.)* Well, that's me. *(Nick gives Aida, then Emma, then Nunzio, a hug.)* So — I'll see you all soon — real soon — so no "good-byes" — okay? No "good-byes."

NUNZIO. Good-bye, Nick.

NICK. Gramps!

NUNZIO. I forgot the rules! *(A beat.)* Good-bye, Nick. *(Nick takes a step toward Frank. Frank keeps his distance.)*

NICK. Gramps, c'mon.

FRANK. *Tengo famiglia, Nicola. Tengo famiglia.* You know what that means? *(Nick nods "yes." Car horn blows again. Frank hugs him, hard and quick.)* Go. *(Nick begins to exit.)*

AIDA. Call us when your plane lands!

EMMA. But don't spend any money!

NUNZIO. Just let the phone ring twice!

NICK. You're all really something, you know that? *(A beat. Nick turns towards them.)* I, uh, hope you all know — I have to do this. I have to … *(He cannot go on. Car horn beeps. Nick exits. Emma and Aida go onto the porch and wave good-bye.)*

AIDA. I love you, Nicholas! *(We hear the car pull away. They watch it go for a moment, then reenter the living room and sit. A long beat.)* Who's hungry?

FRANK. He's gone. How can you think of food now? *(A beat.)* Maybe just some provolone. *(Aida exits.)* Everybody goes. *(A spot on Nick.)*

NICK. *(To audience.)* I caught my flight, and six hours later I was in Seattle, my new home. And two days later, a fifteen-pound lasagna arrived for me in the mail. My new job? Loved it. More responsibility, more challenging. And within a month, I started dating this account executive from my office, Theresa, who I immediately knew was pretty special. Two months later, I flew back to my grandparents — to attend the funeral of my grandfather, Nunzio. He died from prostate cancer which had spread to his liver and kidneys. My grandmother told me they had known about it before I moved, but they thought it wasn't right to burden me with it. Burden me? How could they not have said anything? Anything at all? If any one of them did — no question — I would've stayed.

AIDA. *(To audience.)* A couple of years after Nicholas left, my Frank — my baby — passed on. Emma and I shared dinner together every day for nearly a year after that, until she, too, suffered a severe stroke. God rest them. I still cook two meals a day for myself, and I make something a little special on Sunday. And I still see my Nicholas. Because of his job, he flies to New York often, and he always pays his grandmother a visit. *(Nick enters the living room.)*

NICK. Nan, it's me!

AIDA. Nicholas!

NICK. How are ya, Nan! God, it's hot in here!

AIDA. Oh, you look hungry. Let me put the ravioli in the water.

NICK. Nan, I'm so sorry, the conference ran long, I can only stay a few minutes, I have to catch this flight —

AIDA. The water's boiling, it'll just take a —

NICK. No Nan, let's not eat. Let's just sit and talk — I have something to tell you.

AIDA. The ravioli looks beautiful.

NICK. Nan, I'm moving.

AIDA. Oh, Nicholas. Back home?

NICK. To Portland. I got another job — a vice president — a wonderful promotion.

AIDA. Theresa's going with you?

NICK. No, she's got to stay in Seattle for now.

AIDA. But you're engaged?

NICK. Right. Well, we'll fly back and forth on weekends, Nan. It's called a commuter relationship. It's very modern, very annoying. Nan, I had this idea — move with me to Portland. It's actually a beautiful city.

AIDA. Nicholas?

NICK. Your whole life you've lived here, Nan. Taking care of Grandpa all the time. Come to Portland. You won't have to take care of anybody. If you want, I'll take you out to eat every night. I'd love to give that to you, Nan. There's no one here for you anymore.

AIDA. Nicholas, do you know where I always wanted to go for years and years? Atlantic City. That's right, Nunz and Emma always came back with such stories, but your grandfather, he would have no part of such a fancy place. But one day, I left him a plate in the icebox and I went. And you know what? I didn't like it. No, the whole time I was there, I was wishing I was back home, taking care of your grandfather. I had to take care of him, Nicholas. He needed me to — so much. How many people can get to be my age and can say that — that there was someone who needed them that much. I can say that, Nicholas. I can't go. Not from here. Your grandfather built this house for me. How can I go? Stay for dinner. Please.

NICK. Okay. Okay. *(Aida exits into the kitchen.)* Not long after, I achieved what my grandparents considered the greatest accomplishment known to man: I married. *Tengo famiglia.* And now, when Theresa and I sit home in Portland, awaiting the birth of our first child, my mind often wanders back to those few final days spent with my grandparents. And I wish I could neatly sum up who they were and what they meant to me and how they fit into the puzzle of my life. But instead, what is most clear to me, is that my grandparents worked every day of their lives to ensure that their family would be more educated and successful than them. *(Aida enters, setting the table.)* But what they didn't foresee was that they would elevate me to a life so far removed from their own that they could never quite comprehend who I had become or how I would continue their legacy. And when I looked back at them, I, too, saw only a vague reflection of myself. Still, they let me go — they got me to laugh — and to this day, I get great food in the mail.

AIDA. Everything came beautiful — didn't it, Nicholas?

End of Play